Nightmare

Keith Fletcher and
Susan Duberley

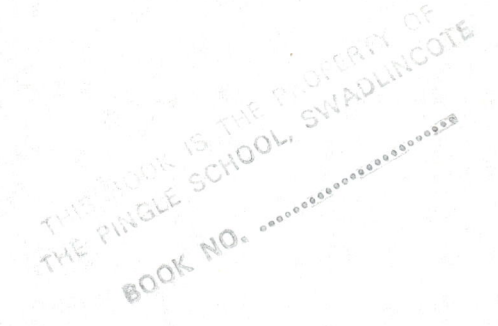

Stanley Thornes (Publishers) Ltd

© Keith Fletcher and Susan Duberley 1984

All rights reserved. No part of this publication may be reproduced or transmitted in any form or by any means, electronic or mechanical, including photocopy, recording, or any information storage and retrieval system, without permission in writing from the publisher or under licence from the Copyright Licensing Agency Limited. Further details of such licences (for reprographic reproduction) may be obtained from the Copyright Licensing Agency Limited, of 90 Tottenham Court Road, London W1P 9HE.

First published 1984 by Hutchinson Education

Reprinted 1991 by
Stanley Thornes (Publishers) Ltd
Ellenborough House
Wellington Street
CHELTENHAM GL50 1YW
England

98   99   00   /   10

British Library Cataloguing in Publication Data

Fletcher, Keith
   Nightmare lake.—(Spirals).
   1. Readers—1950–
   I. Title   II. Duberley, Susan   III. Series
   428.6'2   PE1121

ISBN 0 7487 1026 4

Cover photograph by The Image Bank, London
Cover design by Ned Hoste
Printed and bound in Great Britain at Martin's The Printers, Berwick

1

Once I loved fishing. I loved to sit on the grassy bank with a rod in my hand. If I didn't catch a fish, it didn't matter. It was just good to be in the fresh air. It was good to see the trees and the green grass. Sometimes I would stop watching the float and just lie back and look up at the sky.

How I long for those days now. What I would give to be able to fish again!

You see, I will never be able to fish again. I will never be able to sit by a lake or river. Just to think about water fills me with fear.

It is hard to believe, I know. Only two months ago, I was as happy as a bird. I was free to do all the things I loved doing. I was free to sit by the water for hours on end.

But not any more. Two months ago something happened to me. Now my life is full of fear. Even as I write this down, I know I am not safe.

2

It all started when I went away on holiday. I wanted to go to Dorset. It was a good place for fishing. It was also where my father was born. I had never seen my father. He had left Dorset when he was a young man and died not long after. So I wanted to see where he had lived.

I booked in at a hotel. It was only a small hotel but it was near my father's village. It was also not far from a beautiful lake. When I first saw it, I could hardly wait to start fishing.

I will never forget that first morning of my holiday. It was a lovely day. There was a wood around most of the lake and an island in the middle. At first I just sat down and looked at it all. Then I set up my rods on the bank.

I spent all day fishing by the lake, but I didn't catch anything. That happens sometimes. It doesn't matter. It's all part of the fun of fishing. The main thing is to have a good long rest and feel happy at the end of the day. And that is just how I felt.

Then it began to get dark. Suddenly I did not feel

quite so happy. A strange chill came over me, and I felt afraid. It was a bit like when you have seen a horror film. You feel frightened. Sometimes your mind can play tricks and you think you can see or hear things.

That is how I felt then. I had a feeling I was not alone. I was sure I was being watched. It made me shudder. Somewhere, someone was watching me.

Quickly I pulled in my fishing line. Then I tried to pack up my rods. I say 'tried', because my hands kept shaking. I could not stop them.

I had just finished packing when something made me look up. This time I saw something move. It was behind a tree not far away. Now I was sure of it. Something, or someone was watching me. I did not intend to find out who or what it was. All I wanted was to get away as fast as possible. I knew I would not be happy until I was miles away.

3

I bent down to pick up my fishing tackle. It was then that I saw a shape. It was the shape of a woman. She was standing by the tree where I had first seen something move.

She was young: about seventeen or eighteen perhaps. In the moonlight I could see that she had long fair hair. Her dress was long too, and very white. She was so beautiful that I could not take my eyes away from her. There was something odd about her as well. It seemed to me that she was lost. As I stared at her, I felt she needed help. I felt she needed someone to turn to.

My fear left me. I did not want to go any more. I wanted to get to know this strange girl. I wanted to know what she was doing here.

At first I thought that she might speak to me, but she made no sound. She did not move away but she did not come nearer. Then slowly a smile crept across her face. It was a small, sad smile. I had to get to know her. 'Hello,' I said. This time I was sure she would speak, but again she said nothing.

Yet I could see she was pleased that I had spoken. I could tell from her face.

Picking up my fishing tackle, I began to walk over to her. I wanted to ask her where she lived. As I got nearer, she suddenly darted off. Then she stopped behind a tree and smiled at me. It was as if she was playing a game. I almost felt she wanted me to try and catch her. But when I moved, she ran away.

She moved very quickly, like a wild animal. There were no shoes on her feet and she made no sound. Yet, as she ran behind the tree, I was sure I could hear laughter. Silver laughter. She wanted me to play with her. I was sure of it. Like some child, she wanted me to play 'catch'.

Quickly I dropped my fishing tackle and ran to the tree. If that was what she wanted, then I was going to play. Nothing would stop me.

4

How long the game lasted, I don't know. It was all so odd. There we were, two people, playing like children. We had never spoken. But at the time, it all seemed normal. It was fun.

I couldn't catch her. However hard I tried, she always slipped away. In the end I was tired out. I flopped down under an oak tree just outside the wood. I had to rest.

I looked up, and I saw the girl standing over me. She was laughing at me. Her eyes shone in the moonlight and her hair hung in wisps over her face. She was beautiful. Beautiful but strange.

I had to see her again. I had to get to know her better. 'What is your name?' I asked. I looked up at her, waiting for the answer. But again she said nothing. 'Look,' I said. 'My name is Mark. Please tell me your name.'

Still she said nothing, but this time she did smile a little. So I tried once more. 'All right. Don't tell me your name if you don't want to. But let me buy you a drink. There is a pub near here.'

This time I knew I had said the wrong thing. The smile left the girl's face and she began to look upset. For a moment I thought she was going to turn away. Quickly I said, 'No, I'll tell you what. Let's meet here by the lake tomorrow.' This time the smile came back. I had said the right thing.

I looked down at the grass for a moment. It shone almost silver in the moonlight. When I looked up again the girl had gone. I opened my mouth to call her. Then I remembered: I still didn't know her name.

I rushed to the clump of trees near by. Perhaps she was playing her games again — but no. There was no sign of her. She must have gone.

I lay back down in the grass and stared at the stars. I thought about the girl. I couldn't take my mind away from her. I couldn't wait for the next day. But would she come? She hadn't said she would. That was what was so odd. We had spent all that time together and she had not spoken one word.

At last I got to my feet. I made my way to where I had left my fishing tackle. All the time I was thinking about the girl. In the morning I had just been fishing. It had been the first day of my holiday. Now, at the end of that same first day, I had met the girl. I had played the game of 'catch' and I couldn't wait until tomorrow.

I stopped to take one last look at the lake. It was very still and dark in the moonlight. Suddenly I felt a chill in the air. A feeling of fear began to grip me again. It was the same feeling I had felt before. This time it was so bad that I could hardly breathe. My mouth was dry. I began to panic. I had to get away at all costs.

My mind flew to the girl. Was she still in the wood or had she gone home? Perhaps she was still there and frightened like me. As I rushed away from the lake I kept my eyes scanned for her. I tried to keep calm. Then a cloud passed over the moon and everywhere was dark. Brambles and twigs tore at my face. They seemed almost alive, like the claws of an animal. I hoped the girl was safe at home but as I ran I still looked for her.

I didn't know where I was going. My heart pounded like a hammer in my chest. My body shook with fear. The next moment I crashed into a tree and fell to the ground. Quickly I pulled myself up and started running again.

Then at last I found I was out of the wood. I could see my car in the lane where I had parked it. I jumped in and started the engine. I drove away at great speed.

As I left the lake behind me, I began to feel better. The fear left me. My mind went back to the girl. I hoped she was safe at home. Perhaps I had been selfish? Should I have checked the woods to make sure she was not there?

I could not put her out of my mind. At the same time I remembered the fear I had felt by the lake. Was there a link between the two? Did the girl have something to do with my fear? No, no. I was just mixed up.

At the hotel I walked up and down the room. I could not take the girl out of my mind. I was longing to see her. Yet at the back of my mind I kept remembering the fear by the lake. My mind began to spin. I had to go to bed. With a good sleep I would feel better. Everything is always better after a good sleep.

At least, that is what I thought.

5

I did not sleep very well. I spent most of the night dreaming, then waking up in cold terror. Each time the dream was the same. It was a nightmare. I was in a wood — but it wasn't a real wood. The trees were alive like strange, dark animals. All the time they seemed to be watching me. Their branches twisted around my neck like arms. Whenever I tried to move, the branches pulled tighter and brambles clawed at me.

The girl was in my dream too. I could see her, trapped like me, her large eyes filled with fear. I was trying to get to her, but the trees and brambles stopped me. Then suddenly her face would change and she would laugh a cold, hard laugh. And the branches pulled tighter round my neck. I was just about to die for lack of air when I would wake up.

It was a terrible dream and I lay in the darkness shaking. Then I would fall asleep — and the same dream happened over and over again.

At last I woke to find the bright morning sunlight in my room. I crawled out of bed, trying to forget the dream. Pulling back the bedroom curtains, I looked outside. It was a beautiful day, with the sun shining. I began to feel a bit better.

By the time I had eaten a good breakfast and had drunk three cups of coffee, I felt almost myself again. As I slowly drank my last cup, I thought about the girl. I could not wait for the evening to come. My fears by the lake did not worry me any more. In fact, I couldn't understand why I had run away like that. I would have to stop watching so many horror films!

I didn't feel like fishing that day. I thought I would potter around the village in the morning. It was only a mile from the hotel. Then perhaps I would go for a walk in the afternoon.

I took my time looking around the village. It was very pretty with old, stone cottages and narrow streets. I wished I knew which cottage my father had once lived in. But I hadn't liked to ask Mum. Mum didn't like to talk about Dad much. She had married a year after he had died and I suppose she didn't want to upset my step-father. Still, I enjoyed looking round. I even spent half an hour walking around the church. A few times I passed men digging their front gardens. I thought perhaps they might have known my father when he was young, but I didn't like to stop and ask them. It seemed a bit rude.

Around opening time I popped into a pub on the edge of the village. I ordered some fish and chips in a basket and a pint of beer. As I was waiting, I sat down in a corner of the pub.

I hadn't been there long when a man came over to my table. He was one of the men I had passed in the morning. For a moment he stared at me, then he said: 'Excuse me. You look a bit like someone I knew a long time ago.' I smiled. 'Tom Spenn?' I asked. 'Yes, that's right,' the man said, sitting down at the table. 'You must be his son. You look alike and you sound just the same. What are you doing in this part of the world? What's your Dad up to, these days?' 'Dad died,' I said. 'He died at sea. It was a long time ago, and I wasn't very old. That's really why I came here on holiday. I wanted to see where he had lived. I didn't really know him, you see.'

The man nodded. 'I knew your Dad quite well for a time,' he said. 'But you know how it is. You grow up and start work and grow apart. But we went round a lot as kids.' He grinned. 'We were in the same football team and did some fishing together. And got up to a good few pranks.' I laughed. 'I'd love to hear about them,' I said. 'Let me get you a drink.'

I spent the next half-an-hour talking to the man. His name was Mr Platt. I must say, I felt very lucky that I had bumped into someone who had known my father. I hoped he would ask me round to his house before the end of my holiday, but he didn't. But he did tell me a good place to go for my walk in the afternoon.

As he was about to leave, I stopped him. 'Is there anyone else in the village who knew my father?' I asked. The man shook his head. 'There are one or two,' he said after a moment. 'But I wouldn't look them up, lad, if I were you.' 'Why not?' I asked, surprised. He looked at me for a time. He seemed to be trying to make up his mind about something. In the end he said, 'People round here got a bit angry with your Dad. It wasn't much really. But your father went out with a girl from a village nearby. They went out with each other for a long time. Her name was Miranda. Everyone thought they were going to get married. Then your Dad suddenly left the village. He didn't tell the girl or anything. Well. Everyone was sorry for the girl, that's all. They thought your Dad had treated her badly.' Mr Platt stopped. 'It's nothing to worry about lad,' he said, patting my back. 'Your Dad was a good bloke. Sometimes you just do silly things when you are young.'

Mr Platt smiled. 'I've got to go,' he said. 'I'm on shift. But I'm glad to have met you. I hope you have a good holiday.' He waved as he left the pub. I walked over to the bar and ordered another beer. Then I sat down in the corner for another half-an-hour. I thought about my father and all that Mr Platt had told me.

I didn't want to spend too long walking in the afternoon. After all, I was meeting the girl in the evening and I didn't know what time she might come. She could be at the lake at seven o'clock, or even six. I didn't want to miss her. So I went the way Mr Platt had told me about and took a short cut back to the hotel.

I enjoyed the afternoon. Dorset is a good place for walking. I passed all sorts of roads and lanes that I wanted to go down. In fact, I made up my mind that the next day I would spend my time exploring the area.

When I reached the hotel it was five o'clock. I was too late for tea and too soon for the evening meal. Anyway, I did not want to wait for that. Now that it was so near to meeting the girl, I just wanted to get down to the lake. I knew she wouldn't be there yet, but I could do some fishing while I waited.

The hotel was very good. I was packed up with a large picnic and hot drinks. Soon I was sitting by the edge of the lake, munching sandwiches. Then I lay back in the grass. Fishing was not on my mind.

All I could think about now was the girl. Would she come? Would she remember our meeting? I was so excited, you would think it was my first date.

I had set up my rods by the old boat house this time. From there I could see the small island in the lake. I found myself staring at it from time to time. I was sure I had seen something move. Perhaps there was something on the island.

No. There could not have been. I was seeing things.

I looked at my float. It was hardly moving. The water of the lake was like a sheet of glass. The evening sun shone down on it. Fish do not like bright sunlight. I could see I would not catch anything. I lay back in the grass and shut my eyes. I didn't mind. All I wanted to do was think about the girl.

The hours passed. The evening began to fade into dusk. Still the girl had not come. Sadly I started packing up my fishing tackle. There was no point in waiting any more. She wouldn't come now.

I turned away from the lake. Then from far away I heard a cry. It was a shrill, sad cry. My heart almost stopped. It sounded like a trapped bird or animal. Then my hopes began to rise. Perhaps it was the girl playing one of her games? Perhaps she was here after all?

Quickly I looked around for some sign of her. Was she behind a tree waiting to play catch? Or was there something else there: something waiting to catch me?

Suddenly my fears came back.

7

I started to shiver. The fears of the night before began to return. It was only thinking about the girl that stopped me from running away. I found myself staring at the island again. What made me look I don't know, but this time I was sure I saw something move.

There was something standing at the edge of the small island. Something in white. So that was it. She had been standing on the island watching me all evening. I smiled. So she was playing games again.

Goodness knows how she had got to the island. I looked across at the old boat house. There had been a boat there this afternoon. Perhaps she had gone across on that. I stared into the darkness. The boat was tied up where it always had been. I looked back at the island. The girl was still standing by the edge of the water. She did not move or call, but I could see her white dress in the moonlight.

Quickly I ran to the boat house. I pushed the boat into the water, jumped in and grabbed the oars. As fast as I could I rowed over to the island. The moment I hit the small bank I jumped out. Full of hope and excitement, I rushed to where the girl had been standing.

She wasn't there. My heart sank. There was no sign of her. I ran round every inch of that island and found nothing. It was as if no-one had ever been there.

Slowly and sadly I returned to the boat. There was nothing for it but to go back to the boat house. I didn't know what was happening. This time I knew I had not been seeing things. The girl had been on the island. How she had got off it I didn't know. In the darkness I shook my head. It was all very odd. I began to row back.

I didn't have long to think much about the problem. Not far from the boat I saw a shape in the water. It was a body. Floating all around the body was a dress. I could see in the moonlight that the dress was white.

It was the girl.

Quickly I turned the boat and started to row nearer. What was she doing now? Was she up to her tricks again? Was she swimming in the lake?

At first I thought she would swim away, but she didn't. Then, as I drew closer I could see she was floating with her face down in the water.

There was no time to panic. I had to be quick. I pulled the boat as close to her as I could. Then grabbing hold of her dress, I tried with all my strength to pull the body near the boat. I hoped she was still alive. But how long had she been in the water?

It is hard to remember all that I was thinking at the time. Mainly, I was working out ways of saving her. Having dragged the body near to the boat, I started to try and pull it over the side.

It was then that it happened. I have no words to tell you exactly how it felt. All I can say is that my heart seemed to stop. As I was looking at the body, the head slowly turned round in the water. The girl's eyes shot open. She stared at me. Her eyes were cold and hard and cruel. I was filled with terror. As I looked in horror, her lips parted in an evil smile.

Too late I knew the truth. This was no sweet girl. This was some kind of monster. A monster that wanted to harm me, perhaps kill me.

I had been fooled.

In fear I drew back from the girl, but I was too late. Her arms had lifted from the black water and grabbed me around my neck. She was very strong. I struggled to get free but the cold arms got tighter. She was pulling me over the side. She wanted me in the water.

As the boat began to rock, I slipped. Splash! The next moment I was in the water. Now there was no hope for me — she would drag me down, down into the cold, dark lake.

Already I could feel her pulling me under. Her long, fair hair wrapped around my face and neck. It was like a net pulling tighter all the time. I gasped and choked, and I felt the life bubbling out of me.

As I struggled to get free, I banged against something. It was the boat. In my fear I had forgotten about it. Now I thought, if only I could get back into the boat perhaps I could save myself. Somehow I got my hand over the side. Then with all the strength I could find, I kicked and struggled. With one last pull, I flung myself into the boat.

There was no time to lose. I grabbed an oar and hit out at the creature in the water. Again and again I struck — I smashed at the water in a frenzy. My terror drove me on. I went on hitting the water until I fell into the bottom of the boat. I was tired out; I had to rest.

As I lay there, I waited for the sound of the creature. But there was nothing, just a cold silence. For the moment I was free. For the moment I had won . . . but for how long?

Gritting my teeth, I struggled to my knees. I had to get ready for another attack. I had to see if the body was still there. Holding an oar in my hands, I looked carefully at the water. I was ready to hit out the moment I saw her. I was ready to fight for my life.

But there was nothing there: no dress, no body. All I could see was a mass of tangled weeds floating at the side of the boat. Just a mass of weeds. Nothing more.

9

I know what you are thinking. Perhaps there never had been a body. Perhaps in my fear I had just thought the girl was there. If that is what you think, you are wrong. It had happened all right.

A horrible chill of fear still lay across me. At all costs I had to get away. Quickly I rowed to the bank of the lake. Jumping from the boat, I ran to the car. I didn't take my fishing tackle or picnic things. I was too frightened to bother about that.

As I ran, I thought I heard the girl calling. I didn't turn round. Nothing would have made me stop.

I reached the car and jumped in. As quickly as I could I drove away from the lake. I drove too fast. How it was that I did not crash, I will never know. Perhaps at the time, luck was on my side.

When I reached the hotel I rushed to the bar. I had to have a drink. More than that, I had to be with people. Real people. Warm people.

It didn't take long for the barman to find out what was wrong with me. I was only too pleased to tell someone the story. I didn't think anyone would believe me, but I didn't care. All I wanted was to get it off my chest.

The barman was old and kind. He listened to my story carefully. I didn't miss out anything. I started from the moment I first saw the girl by the lake. As I told my story, the barman didn't say a thing. His face stayed the same. Not once did he look surprised. He just stood and listened to me.

When I had finished, the barman gave me another drink. He said he couldn't explain my story. He could only tell me what he had been told when he moved into this hotel. He said that about thirty years ago a girl had drowned in the lake. She had always been a very happy girl, until the boy she loved had left her. From that time on, she had never been the same. She would sit by the lake and gaze into the water, or run from tree to tree. They used to go there a lot, before he left, and it was as if she was still waiting for him. In the end, she threw herself in.

The barman shook his head. 'Since I've been in this hotel, one or two people have claimed to see her. She looks the same as she always did, they say. Except for one thing. They say there is evil in her eyes. It's almost as if she is still looking for someone, but this time, to get her own back.'

The barman stared at me for a moment. 'That's all I know,' he said. I thanked him very much for telling me the story. I also thanked him for listening to mine. 'There's just one other thing,' I said. 'What was the girl's name?'

He frowned for a moment. 'Miranda, I think,' he said. 'That's it. Miranda. But I can't remember the name of the young man.'

10

Somehow I staggered to my room. I was feeling weak; very weak. It wasn't surprising. What had happened to me that evening had been horrible. Very horrible indeed. On top of that, what I had heard in the bar had shocked me.

It was my father who had gone out with Miranda. And it was my father who had left her. She had never got over it. Because of my father, Miranda had killed herself. She had thrown herself into the lake. I could see now why people had been angry with my father.

I went to the bathroom and ran a bath. I needed to relax. A hot bath would help me do that. I also needed to think.

I lay back and thought about my father. I knew he had drowned at sea. I also knew that everyone thought it was odd at the time. The sea had been calm. He was a good swimmer. On top of that, there had been nothing wrong with the boat. Yet my father had drowned. In the end, people said it was 'one of those things'.

As I lay in the bath, I was not so sure. It was too

odd. Miranda had drowned, my father had drowned, and I had nearly drowned this evening. Suddenly it all seemed clear to me. Miranda had somehow killed my father. It was her way of getting her own back.

Now she wanted more. She had not finished. She would not be happy until she got me, Tom Spenn's son. She had tried once. Would she try again?

It seemed that somehow she had made me come to this village. I thought I had come here to see the place where my father had been born. But was that really why I had come? Perhaps it was Miranda who had made me. Perhaps I had come because Miranda had wanted me to.

The odd thing was that my father had drowned at sea. He hadn't drowned in a lake. Why had Miranda waited for me to visit the lake? Did I have to see it first? Was there some plan to it all?

Now that I had come to the lake, I had seen Miranda. What was more, I knew all about her and my father. I shuddered. Perhaps I had to know all this before she could get me. Perhaps, now that I knew I was to die, she could attack me anywhere.

As I lay in the bath I shivered. The bath was hot, but I felt cold all over. Then the lights went out.

11

Darkness filled the bathroom. I couldn't see anything. I was so frightened I couldn't think. I couldn't take any more. In a panic, I struggled to get out of the bath.

Something hit me in the chest. I was pushed back into the bath. Water splashed everywhere. I was too shocked to cry out: too shocked and frightened.

I felt hands, strong hands on my head. They were pushing me under the water. I wanted to scream but I couldn't. I was choked with fear. The room was filled with a bad smell. The smell was of rotting weeds and slime and mud. It was the smell of death. It was so bad I thought I would be sick.

I kicked and punched at whatever was pushing me down. It was no good. I wasn't winning. I wasn't winning the fight for my life.

The room began to fill with laughter. It seemed to come from everywhere. It sounded like the laughter of a mad woman.

Again and again my head was pushed under water.

I struggled for air. My lungs were bursting. There was a pain in my chest. Water went into my lungs as I tried to suck in air. My head throbbed.

Miranda had come to claim me.

As I was kicking weakly, I felt something twisting round my foot. It was the chain holding the plug. Somehow I jerked it. The plug came out. The bathwater slipped away. The plug had saved my life.

The laughter in the bathroom turned to a scream. Miranda was howling with rage. As the howl became softer, I could feel Miranda's hold on me become weaker.

Suddenly I was free. There was no sound in the room. I knew Miranda had gone. I lay there gasping, drinking in the air. I was shaking with fear. My life was turning into a nightmare.

Somehow I dragged myself out of the bath and switched on the light. The brightness made my eyes hurt. For a moment I shut them. When I opened them again I could hardly believe what I saw.

The room was in a terrible mess. There was water all over the floor. The walls were thick with slime and mud. More than that, when I looked at my body I saw it was covered with scratches. They were deep scratches and they were bleeding badly.

I looked weakly into the bath. It was empty. But in the plug hole there was a long strand of weed. And tangled up in it was one long blonde hair.

I knew then that there was no hope. I would never get away from her. My life would never be my own again.

You see, I know that Miranda will get me in the end. She will follow me, just as she did my father. Then one day she will trap me. Until then, the nightmare of the lake will never leave me.

That is why I don't go fishing any more. That is why I am afraid.

What is more, I can never go near water. Where there is water, there will always be Miranda. She will be waiting for me and watching me. If I do one thing wrong she will be there, ready for me. In the end she will claim me, just as she did my father.

So you see, I still have a date with Miranda ... but when and where, I don't know.